THE ... OF
DISCOVERY

by Lisa Moore

Harcourt
SCHOOL PUBLISHERS

Printed in China

ISBN 10: 0-15-350563-x
ISBN 13: 978-0-15-350563-8

Ordering Options
ISBN 10: 0-15-350335-1 (Grade 5 Below-Level Collection)
ISBN 13: 978-0-15-350335-1 (Grade 5 Below-Level Collection)
ISBN 10: 0-15-357564-6 (package of 5)
ISBN 13: 978-0-15-357564-8 (package of 5)

11 12 13 14 15   0940   12 11 10

Back in 1803, President Thomas Jefferson asked two men, Meriwether Lewis and William Clark, to find a way across North America to the Pacific Ocean. Lewis and Clark started out near St. Louis, Missouri. They led a group of about thirty called the Corps of Discovery. It took them two years to get to the Pacific Coast and back. The trip was very long and very dangerous. When they left, many people thought they would never return.

Their journey is one of the most famous journeys in American history. Today, the whole 3,700-mile (5,955 km) trail is a national park. It is called the Lewis and Clark Historic Trail. Every year, thousands of people follow this path.

Today many visitors begin with the Museum of Westward Expansion in St. Louis. The museum is under the Gateway Arch. The Arch is 630 feet (192 m) high! Visitors see exhibits about all kinds of explorers, from Lewis and Clark to the Apollo astronauts. Thirty-three giant photographs showing places all along the Lewis and Clark Trail hang in the museum. Each year, thousands of visitors study these pictures intently before they begin their long trek.

Fort Osage

Most people drive cars along the Lewis and Clark Historic Trail. Others bike. Still, others hike. All along the way, signs point visitors north and west. At first, visitors follow the Missouri River. The Corps of Discovery traveled in boats on the river. In some spots, they had to carry the boats over rough terrain, around rapids and waterfalls. Today people have it easy, gliding along a smooth highway in their cars.

After about 240 miles (386 km), visitors come to Fort Osage in Sibley, Missouri. On his way west, William Clark noted this spot as a good place for a fort. In 1808, he came back to build the fort. Now it's a museum. It looks exactly like it did when the fort was first built, and the guides dress as people did back then. Groups of people act out military drills at this fort. Their acting makes it all seem real!

5

Just like Lewis and Clark, people follow the river from Missouri into Iowa. There they can camp in one of many Lewis and Clark state parks. Every year, the Iowa park holds a Lewis and Clark Festival. Visitors eat buffalo burgers and dance to fiddle music.

One popular sight at the Iowa park is a model of the keelboat that Lewis and Clark used. This boat was 55 feet (17 m) long. It carried men and supplies. Lewis and Clark went upriver against the current, and that boat was heavy. Sometimes the men had to walk along the shore and drag the boat with ropes. What an ordeal that must have been!

The Missouri River and the cornfields seem to go on forever! After long hours of driving, visitors cross the state line into South Dakota. Here, visitors will see rolling hills and herds of buffalo—sometimes at very close range! Several groups of Native Americans, including the Sioux, lived in this part of South Dakota during the time of Lewis and Clark's journey. Many of their descendants, like the Lakota, still live here today.

Many people who follow the trail today enjoy camping. There are many places to camp along the way. For example, people can camp on South Dakota's Lake Oahe. For people who like to fish, this lake is a real asset.

At Fort Mandan, in Washburn, North Dakota, Lewis and Clark met Sacagawea. She was a Shoshone Indian princess who helped the Corps of Discovery. She earned their esteem as a guide and translator. A statue of Sacagawea stands in Bismarck, the capital of North Dakota.

There are so many places to see and visit along the trail. Many people enjoy seeing the Knife River Indian Villages. These villages were once the homes of Hidatsa Indians. The Hidatsa lived in earth lodges, which were round houses covered with dirt and grass. Today people can go inside these earth lodges and learn about the people that used to live there. Even if it rained profusely, the lodges kept people dry.

In New Town, North Dakota, the Three Tribes Museum celebrates the Mandan, Hidatsa, and Arikara people. There visitors may see very old beaded items that were made by members of the three tribes.

As travelers hit the road again, they approach the border of North Dakota and Montana. When he passed this way, Meriwether Lewis wrote that the land was covered with buffalo, elk, and antelope. Today there are far fewer animals, but you can still spot some from your car as you pass.

Karl Bodmer's "Herds of Bison and Elk on the Upper Missouri"

Clark's name as he carved it into
Pompeys Pillar

Once Lewis and Clark reached the Pacific
Ocean, they had to come back, of course. On
the way back, William Clark chose a different route
through southern Montana. Many visitors get off
the westbound trail and drive—or ride or walk—
some of Clark's return trail.

If they take Clark's trail, they get to see Pompeys
Pillar National Monument. The Pillar is a giant
round rock that rises 200 feet (61 m) straight up.
Clark called it "remarkable." He named the rock
after Sacagawea's baby son, Pompey. The most
amazing thing about Pompeys Pillar is that Clark
carved his name into it. It is still there!

The westbound trail meets the eastbound trail at Great Falls, Montana. Great Falls gets its name from the four sets of waterfalls there: Great Falls, Horseshoe Falls, Rainbow Falls, and Black Eagle Falls.

The Corps of Discovery faced a lot of peril at this place. There were dangerous rapids that went on for 20 miles (32 km). Many members of the Corps were sick, and they had to carry their canoes and all their things past the falls and rapids. In one afternoon, Lewis faced down a bear, a mountain cat, a wolverine, and three buffalo!

We know all of this because Lewis and Clark wrote journals nearly every day while they were away. In their journals, they drew sketches and wrote stories. We still have their journals today.

At this point, visitors drive along the Salmon River through the Weippe Prairie in Idaho. Most of the Corps of Discovery arrived at Weippe starving and sick. It was dismal. Then they met the Nez Perce Indians, who fed and protected them.

Moving on, most visitors want to see Hat Rock State Park in Oregon. Hat Rock is another giant stone outcrop. It looks like—you guessed it—a hat! Clark named it in 1805.

In Stevenson, Washington, travelers visit the Columbia Gorge Interpretive Center. Meriwether Lewis's mother is there! Not really, but the woman who plays her does a great job.

As the trail begins to reach its end, people drive along the Columbia River to the Pacific Ocean. It's hard to imagine what the Corps of Discovery felt when they finally saw the ocean. They must have been very happy and very tired. The truth is, they had a hard winter ahead. Then they had to travel the entire way back east. However, they reached their goal—and they returned home to tell the story.

It takes about three weeks to drive the Lewis and Clark Historic Trail, but it is a journey that people never forget. It's a way to relive history and discover—for yourself—a historical journey that helped shape this country.

Think Critically

1. How do you think the author feels about the Lewis and Clark Historic Trail? How can you tell?

2. Why do people still follow this trail, 200 years after Lewis and Clark's journey?

3. What do you think were the greatest challenges that Lewis and Clark faced on their journey to the Pacific?

4. Write several sentences to summarize this book, *The Corps of Discovery*.

5. What image or detail described in this book do you find most interesting? Why?

 Social Studies

Map the Route Look at a map of the United States and trace the Lewis and Clark Historic Trail as it is described in this book. How many of the places mentioned in the book can you find on the map? Using the map's legend, figure out approximately how many miles are between each stop on the trail.

School-Home Connection Could you spend three weeks in a car with your family, driving over 3,700 miles (5,955 km)? With a family member, discuss such a long trek and how—or if!—your family could handle it.

Word Count: 1,252 (with graphic 1,264)